MIND GAMES

MIND GAMES

The Psychology of Influence and Persuasion

B. VINCENT

QuillQuest Publishers

CONTENTS

Chapter 1: Introduction to Influence and Persuasion

Figuring out the Force of Impact

In our advanced world, impact penetrates each aspect of our lives, frequently working quietly underneath our cognizant mindfulness. From the ads that immerse our screens to the suggestions of our companions and partners, the powers of impact shape our choices and ways of behaving in significant ways. This section sets the stage by enlightening the inescapable idea of impact, offering bits of knowledge into how it works and why it holds such influence over us. By understanding the components of impact, perusers will acquire a more profound appreciation for its effect and figure out how to explore the perplexing trap of powerful powers that encompass them.

The Brain research Behind Influence

Welcome to the internal activities of influence. Here, we set out on an excursion into the complicated domain of human brain research, where secret predispositions, subliminal signs, and strong social elements unite to shape our choices. Drawing from many years of exploration in brain research, mental science, and social financial matters, this part reveals the basic rules that drive viable influence. From the inconspicuous impact of correspondence to the significant effect of social verification, we investigate the intriguing interaction between our brains and the enticing messages that encompass us. By digging into the mental components at play, perusers will acquire significant experiences into the workmanship and study of influence, enabling them to use these standards with more noteworthy adequacy in their own and proficient lives.

The Morals of Impact

As we venture further into the domain of impact and influence, we are defied with significant moral inquiries that request our consideration. In this part, we wrestle with the ethical ramifications of employing the influential ability. What recognizes moral influence from control? How would we explore the scarce difference between affecting others and regarding their independence? Through interesting conversations and moral quandaries, we analyze the complicated exchange among influence and morals. Drawing upon philosophical structures and genuine models, we go up against the difficulties of exploring powerful correspondence with trustworthiness and compassion. By drawing in with these moral contemplations, perusers are prepared to explore the perplexing scene of impact with clearness and heart, guaranteeing that their enticing endeavors are grounded in standards of regard, straightforwardness, and moral obligation.

Setting the Stage

Before we set out on our excursion through the complexities of impact and influence, laying out a strong foundation is fundamental. In this section, we spread out the guide for our investigation, depicting the key goals, degree, and design of our request. By giving a reasonable outline of what lies ahead, perusers can situate themselves inside the more extensive scene of the book and comprehend how every section adds to our overall objectives. Furthermore, we offer bits of knowledge into the systems and rules that will direct our assessment, planning perusers to dig into the rich embroidered artwork of mental experiences and pragmatic techniques that look for them. With the stage set, perusers are prepared to leave on an extraordinary excursion of disclosure, strengthening, and dominance in the domain of impact and influence.

Chapter 2: The Art of Persuasive Communication

Making Convincing Messages

In the complicated dance of influence, the words we pick and how we approach our messages employ a significant impact over their viability. This part dives into the specialty of creating convincing messages, investigating the unobtrusive subtleties of language and show that can have a significant effect in catching consideration and influencing minds.

Language is something other than an instrument for correspondence; it is a vehicle for influence. Via cautiously choosing our words, we can bring out strong feelings, trigger firmly established wants, and tap into the fundamental inspirations of our crowd. Whether it's using distinctive symbolism, convincing narrating, or key requests to rationale and feeling, powerful communicators comprehend how to tailor their messages to resound with their crowd on an instinctive level.

Moreover, the manner in which we outline our messages can essentially affect how they are gotten. Whether outlining an issue decidedly to feature expected gains or adversely to underline likely misfortunes, the outlining impact can shape discernments and impact dynamic in significant ways.

By excelling at creating convincing messages, communicators can saddle the full force of language and outlining to charm their crowd, move activity, and accomplish their enticing goals. Through a blend of imagination, sympathy, and key reasoning, they can create messages that resound profoundly with their crowd, having an enduring impression and driving significant change.

The Job of Nonverbal Correspondence

In the orchestra of influence, nonverbal signals create a critical tune, frequently talking stronger than words themselves. This part digs into the mind boggling universe of nonverbal correspondence, investigating the significant effect of non-verbal communication, tone, and looks on the convincingness of a message.

While our words pass on the unequivocal substance of our message, our nonverbal signs frequently pass on the basic feelings, perspectives, and aims that shape how our message is gotten. From the certain stance of a charming speaker to the certifiable warmth of a genuine grin, nonverbal signs can upgrade the believability of a communicator and encourage trust and compatibility with the crowd.

Besides, nonverbal correspondence fills in as an amazing asset for influence, permitting communicators to pass on unpretentious messages and impact the discernments and perspectives of their crowd. Whether it's using signals to underscore central issues, vocal expressions to convey energy and conviction, or eye to eye connection to lay out association and commitment, gifted communicators comprehend how to use nonverbal prompts to upgrade the influence of their message.

By sharpening their attention to nonverbal correspondence and becoming amazing at its essential use, communicators can intensify the effect of their message, charming their crowd and moving activity with each motion, articulation, and sound. Through a blend of sympathy, legitimacy, and careful presence, they can manufacture further associations and evoke more noteworthy receptivity to their convincing endeavors, at last accomplishing their ideal results with elegance and impact.

Building Validity

In the domain of influence, validity is the cash of trust, the foundation whereupon compelling correspondence is fabricated. This part dives into the fundamental techniques for laying out and upgrading validity in correspondence, furnishing communicators with the apparatuses they need to motivate certainty and cultivate trust in their crowd.

Believability incorporates a range of properties, including skill, dependability, and generosity. Communicators who have aptitude in their field are seen as learned and skilled, loaning weight to their contentions and proposals. Similarly, unwavering quality — exhibited through consistency, reliability, and honesty — reinforces the believability of a communicator, consoling the crowd of their truthfulness and dependability.

Additionally, generosity — appeared through warmth, sympathy, and real worry for the government assistance of others — encourages a profound association with the crowd, improving the agreeability and convincingness of the communicator. By developing generosity, communicators can lay out compatibility and sympathy with their crowd, establishing a favorable climate for influence to happen.

Through a blend of skill, consistency, and empathy, communicators can fabricate believability and entrust with their crowd, establishing the groundwork for successful influence. By epitomizing these traits and legitimately interfacing with their crowd, communicators can manufacture enduring connections based on shared regard and understanding, at last engaging them to accomplish their enticing targets with honesty and impact.

Defeating Obstruction

In the field of influence, opposition frequently remains as an impressive hindrance between the communicator and their ideal result. This part investigates powerful strategies for tending to distrust and complaints, enabling communicators to explore obstruction and encourage receptivity to their messages.

Opposition can take many structures, going from inside and out doubt to unobtrusive reluctance or lack of concern. Anything its pretense, compelling communicators comprehend that opposition is a characteristic reaction to convincing endeavors and should be met with persistence, sympathy, and vital influence.

One powerful strategy for beating obstruction is to effectively pay attention to the worries and complaints of the crowd, recognizing their point of view and approving their sentiments. By exhibiting sympathy and understanding, communicators can fabricate compatibility and entrust with their crowd, making an establishment for significant exchange and influence.

Also, communicators can utilize convincing procedures, for example, reevaluating protests, giving proof and tributes, or offering motivations or awards to address the worries of the crowd and lighten their opposition. By introducing powerful claims and tending to potential protests prudently, communicators can construct a more grounded case for their message and improve the probability of influence.

Through a mix of undivided attention, compassion, and key influence, communicators can beat obstruction and encourage receptivity to their messages, at last accomplishing their convincing targets with beauty and viability. By drawing in with the worries and protests of their crowd with truthfulness and legitimacy, communicators can assemble trust and believability, making ready for significant influence and positive results.

Chapter 3: Leveraging Social Influence

The Force of Social Confirmation

In the many-sided dance of influence, barely any powers use as much impact as the peculiarity of social confirmation. This segment digs into the significant effect of meaningful gestures and gathering conduct on individual navigation, enlightening how the activities and assessments of others shape our discernments and ways of behaving in manners both unpretentious and significant.

At its center, social confirmation works on the guideline of congruity — the inclination for people to adjust their perspectives and ways of behaving to those of the gathering. Whether it's the clamoring café with a line out the entryway or the viral virtual entertainment post with huge number of preferences and offers, we are continually barraged with prompts that signal the prominence and attractiveness of specific decisions and ways of behaving.

However, social evidence is something other than a result of congruity; it is likewise an incredible asset for influence. By exhibiting the way of behaving and assessments of others, communicators can take advantage of the natural human longing to fit in and have a place, utilizing the convincing force of social verification to influence suppositions, shape discernments, and impact conduct.

From tributes and supports to client surveys and virtual entertainment powerhouses, social verification appears in heap shapes, each with its remarkable capacity to reinforce the convincingness of a message. By understanding the components of social verification and figuring out how to tackle its power really, communicators can enhance the effect of their enticing endeavors, making a gradually expanding influence that reverberates a long ways past individual cooperations and drives significant change in mentalities and ways of behaving.

Authority and Compliance

In the domain of social impact, the presence of power figures applies a significant effect on individual way of behaving, frequently prompting dutifulness and consistence even notwithstanding upright uncertainty or moral difficulties. This part digs into the mind boggling elements of power and acquiescence, drawing experiences from original mental tests, for example, the Milgram try and the Stanford jail review.

Through these milestone studies, we gain a sobering comprehension of the degree to which people will submit to power figures, in any event, when it clashes with their own ethical standards or feeling of good and bad. From the stunning acquiescence to orders to direct electric shocks in the Milgram trial to the upsetting plunge into oppression and maltreatment of force in the Stanford jail study, these examinations uncover the dull underside of human instinct and the defenselessness of people to the impact of power.

However, while the discoveries of these trials might be disrupting, they likewise offer significant examples for understanding and moderating the hurtful impacts of expert on conduct. By focusing a light on the components fundamental compliance, we can foster methodologies for opposing excessive impact, encouraging decisive reasoning, and advancing moral dynamic notwithstanding authority.

Through a mix of mindfulness, schooling, and strengthening, people can figure out how to explore the complicated exchange among power and dutifulness with more noteworthy independence and trustworthiness, at last guaranteeing that their activities line up with their qualities and standards, instead of indiscriminately following the directs of power figures.

Making Impact Organizations

Inside the texture of social collaborations lies a strong power: impact organizations. This segment digs into the complicated elements of informal communities and relational connections, investigating how powerhouses and assessment pioneers can use their social cash-flow to impact change.

Impact networks are networks of associations that tight spot people together, forming the progression of data, thoughts, and ways of behaving inside a local area or gathering. At the core of these organizations are forces to be reckoned with — people who have an unbalanced measure of impact and employ the ability to influence suppositions, shape insights, and drive conduct change.

Whether it's the pattern setting design blogger whose proposals direct the most recent styles or the local area pioneer whose supports influence political loyalties, powerhouses assume a crucial part in forming the perspectives and ways of behaving of people around them. By excellence of their societal position, skill, or charm, forces to be reckoned with can apply a gravitational draw on the sentiments and activities of others, catalyzing fountains of impact that echo through whole informal communities.

Yet, impact networks are not exclusively the space of big names and well known people; they exist inside each local area and gathering, from families and companionship circles to working environments and on-line networks. By understanding the elements of impact organizations and distinguishing key hubs and connectors inside their own groups of friends, people can saddle the force of social cash-flow to enhance their enticing endeavors and impact significant change in mentalities and ways of behaving.

Through a blend of relationship-building, correspondence, and key correspondence, people can develop impact inside their own organizations, situating themselves as confided in wellsprings of data and direction and utilizing their social funding to rouse activity and drive positive results.

Collective vibes

In the mind boggling embroidery of social impact, collective vibes assume a urgent part in molding perspectives, ways of behaving, and dynamic cycles. This segment dives into the complexities of gathering conduct, similarity, and mindless conformity, revealing insight into how the elements of gatherings can either work with or repress successful influence procedures.

Bunches have a novel arrangement of elements that impact individual conduct in significant ways. From the strain to adjust to the standards and assumptions for the gathering to the inclination for bunch individuals to look for agreement and stay away from struggle, the elements of gatherings can apply a strong impact on the mentalities and ways of behaving of their individuals.

Similarity — the propensity for people to change their perspectives and ways of behaving to line up with those of the gathering — is quite possibly of the most legitimate peculiarity in friendly brain research. Whether it's the friend strain to adjust to style or the longing to find a place with a specific gathering, congruity can apply a strong draw on individual way of behaving, molding choices and activities in unpretentious and frequently oblivious ways.

Be that as it may, while similarity can cultivate union and participation inside gatherings, it can likewise prompt mindless conformity — a peculiarity portrayed by a tight spotlight on agreement and a hesitance to think about elective perspectives. Mindless compliance can smother imagination, stifle contradiction, and lead to unfortunate independent direction, eventually subverting the viability of influence endeavors.

By understanding the elements of gathering conduct and figuring out how to explore the fragile harmony among similarity and free reasoning, communicators can use the force of gatherings to improve the enticement of their messages while preparing for the traps of oblivious compliance. Through a mix of sympathy, decisive reasoning, and key correspondence, they can tackle the aggregate insight and impact of gatherings to drive positive change and cultivate significant results.

Chapter 4: Cognitive Biases and Persuasion Tactics

Grasping Mental Predispositions

In the maze of the human brain, mental predispositions prowl, quietly forming our discernments and choices in manners that frequently make no sense and reason. This segment dives into the captivating universe of mental inclinations, revealing the normal mental alternate ways and perceptual mutilations that impact our reasoning and conduct.

Mental predispositions are the aftereffect of our cerebrum's noteworthy effectiveness in handling data, permitting us to explore the intricacies of the world effortlessly. Be that as it may, this effectiveness includes some major disadvantages, as it can mislead us when confronted with equivocal or questionable circumstances.

From the tendency to look for predictable answers, which drives us to search out data that affirms our current convictions, to the accessibility heuristic, which makes us misjudge the significance of data that is promptly accessible in our memory, mental predispositions manifest in heap shapes, each with its remarkable effect on our dynamic cycles.

In any case, while mental predispositions might incline us toward blunders in judgment and direction, they additionally present open doors for influence. By understanding the mental easy routes and perceptual mutilations that support these inclinations, communicators can tailor their messages to line up with the mental cycles of their crowd, improving the probability of influence.

Through a mix of sympathy, knowledge, and vital correspondence, communicators can use mental inclinations to make messages that reverberate profoundly with their crowd, taking advantage of the subliminal drivers of human way of behaving and getting wanted reactions with accuracy and viability.

Taking advantage of Mental Triggers

Inside the complex embroidery of human brain research lie a heap of triggers — both close to home and mental — that can be saddled to summon wanted reactions and ways of behaving. This segment dives into the domain of mental triggers, investigating how communicators can handily employ these triggers to dazzle their crowd and impact their direction.

Close to home triggers, like trepidation, bliss, outrage, and want, significantly affect our insights and activities, frequently driving us to answer intuitively and imprudently. By taking advantage of these base feelings, communicators can summon strong profound reactions in their crowd, making a well established association that reverberates on an instinctive level.

Mental triggers, then again, appeal to our sane resources and scholarly interest, provoking us to participate in more profound reflection and examination. Whether it's using indisputable cases, interesting inquiries, or novel experiences, communicators can animate the mental resources of their crowd, inciting them to think about new points of view and conceivable outcomes.

By decisively joining close to home and mental triggers, communicators can make messages that reverberate on different levels, drawing in both the heart and the psyche of their crowd. Whether looking to motivate activity, incite thought, or cultivate compassion, the wise utilization of mental triggers can intensify the convincingness of a message, having an enduring impression and driving significant change.

Bumping Conduct

In the domain of influence, now and again the most remarkable impact comes not from unmistakable pressure or control, but rather from unobtrusive bumps that tenderly aide conduct towards wanted results. This segment dives into the entrancing universe of social bumps, investigating how communicators can utilize unobtrusive intercessions to impact decision-production without limiting opportunity of decision.

Conduct prods influence standards from social financial matters and brain science to guide people towards explicit activities or ways of behaving. Whether it's modifying the format of a supermarket to support better food decisions or outlining choices such that features the default decision, pushes work by unpretentiously changing the setting in which choices are made, making specific ways of behaving more notable, helpful, or socially attractive.

The excellence of pokes lies in their capacity to impact conduct without depending on pressure or control. Rather than forcing limitations or commands, pokes offer people the opportunity to settle on their own decisions while delicately directing them towards choices that line up with their objectives and values.

By understanding the standards of conduct prods and figuring out how to apply them really, communicators can impact dynamic in different settings, from elevating better ways of life to empowering ecologically maintainable ways of behaving. Through a blend of inventiveness, sympathy, and vital reasoning, they can plan mediations that bump people towards positive results, enabling them to settle on decisions that benefit themselves and society in general.

Checking Predispositions

In the perplexing dance of influence, mental predispositions can frequently introduce considerable obstructions to compelling correspondence. This segment dives into methodologies for neutralizing the impacts of mental inclinations, enabling communicators to conquer obstruction and cultivate more normal dynamic cycles.

Mental predispositions emerge from the inborn limits of our mental design, driving us to go astray from reasonableness and rationale in unsurprising ways. From the securing predisposition, which makes us depend too vigorously on the principal snippet of data we experience, to the radiance impact, which drives us to make uncalled-for suspicions in light of a solitary trademark, mental predispositions can contort our discernments and decisions in unobtrusive and frequently deceptive ways.

Nonetheless, while mental predispositions might present difficulties to compelling influence, they are not unrealistic impediments. By understanding the components fundamental mental inclinations and figuring out how to perceive their impact, communicators can foster techniques for relieving their belongings and encouraging more sane dynamic cycles.

One compelling methodology is to furnish people with precise and fair data, permitting them to settle on additional educated choices liberated from the impact of mental inclinations. Furthermore, communicators can support decisive reasoning and incredulity, engaging people to scrutinize their suspicions and assess data all the more equitably.

By furnishing themselves with information and mindfulness, communicators can explore the perplexing scene of mental predispositions with more noteworthy adequacy, guaranteeing that their enticing endeavors are grounded in standards of reason, proof, and respectability. Through a blend of schooling, compassion, and vital correspondence, they can engage people to oppose the draw of mental predispositions and pursue choices that are really lined up with their qualities and objectives.

Chapter 5: Persuasion in Practice

Promoting and Publicizing

Welcome to the universe of influence in the commercial center, where each notice, trademark, and item situation is painstakingly created to catch consideration, summon want, and drive purchaser conduct. This segment digs into the domain of showcasing and publicizing, taking apart the powerful strategies utilized by sponsors to impact purchaser decisions and drive deals.

At its center, promoting is tied in with narrating — making stories that reverberate with customers' yearnings, wants, and values. Whether it's using convincing visuals, reminiscent language, or optimistic informing, publicists look to manufacture a profound association with their crowd, taking advantage of their most profound cravings and fears to constrain activity.

Yet, influence in advertising goes past simple narrating; it additionally includes the essential utilization of mental standards to impact purchaser conduct. From the shortage impact, which makes a need to get going by featuring restricted accessibility, to the correspondence standard, which urges shoppers to respond liberality by making a buy, sponsors influence a scope of mental predispositions and influence strategies to shape insights and drive buying choices.

By understanding the procedures and techniques utilized by advertisers, customers can turn out to be more sagacious and knowing in their utilization propensities, perceiving when they are being impacted and pursuing more educated decisions thus. Through a blend of decisive reasoning, mindfulness, and media education, people can explore the powerful scene of showcasing and publicizing with more prominent certainty and independence, guaranteeing that their buying choices line up with their qualities and needs.

Exchange and Impact

Exchange is the specialty of influence in real life, where clashing interests meet, and gatherings try to agree. This part digs into the domain of discussion and impact, investigating the procedures and strategies that empower moderators to accomplish their ideal results while protecting connections and generosity.

At its center, discussion is tied in with settling on something worth agreeing on and connecting contrasts through discourse and split the difference. Successful moderators grasp the significance of building affinity, undivided attention, and compassion, as these relational abilities establish the groundwork for trust and coordinated effort.

Influence assumes a focal part in exchange, as mediators look to convince their partners to consent to their terms and concessions. Whether it's using powerful language, outlining methods, or concessions and motivations, moderators influence a scope of strategies to impact the insights and choices of their partners.

However, exchange isn't just about getting what you need; it's likewise about making worth and cultivating mutual benefit results. By embracing a cooperative outlook and zeroing in on shared interests and targets, mediators can expand the potential for common addition and construct reasonable connections in view of trust and collaboration.

Through a mix of readiness, vital reasoning, and compelling correspondence, mediators can explore the intricacies of exchange with expertise and artfulness, accomplishing their targets while safeguarding connections and encouraging long haul achievement. Whether arranging an agreement, settling a contention, or trying to propel their inclinations, people can use the standards of influence to accomplish ideal results and fabricate more grounded, more cooperative connections simultaneously.

Political Influence

Governmental issues is the milestone of thoughts, where contending stories conflict and competitors strive for the hearts and brains of citizens. This segment digs into the domain of political influence, inspecting the systems and strategies utilized by lawmakers and activists to influence general assessment and assemble support for their plans.

At its center, political influence is tied in with outlining issues and forming discernments, as competitors try to situate themselves as the most ideal decision to address electors' interests and goals. Whether it's using convincing manner of speaking, close to home requests, or designated informing, political communicators mean to motivate trust, certainty, and faithfulness among their allies.

However, political influence isn't exclusively about winning decisions; it's likewise about assembling support for strategy drives and social causes. From grassroots getting sorted out and local area commitment to computerized promotion and virtual entertainment crusades, political activists influence a scope of strategies to construct alliances, intensify voices, and impact significant change.

Nonetheless, political influence isn't without its moral contemplations and difficulties. From the expansion of falsehood and phony news to the control of feelings and predispositions, the strategies utilized in political influence can at times subvert the vote based process and dissolve public confidence in organizations.

By understanding the standards of political influence and figuring out how to fundamentally assess political messages and stories, electors can turn out to be more educated and drawn in members in the political cycle, guaranteeing that their voices are heard and their inclinations addressed. Through a blend of media education, decisive reasoning, and community commitment, people can explore the intricacies of political influence with certainty and organization, eventually adding to a more dynamic and comprehensive vote based system.

Individual Impact

In the field of individual and expert connections, influence is an essential expertise that can shape the course of connections and results. This segment investigates the use of influence procedures in regular communications, offering bits of knowledge into how people can use influence to accomplish their objectives and improve their connections.

Viable influence in private collaborations is grounded in standards of sympathy, undivided attention, and compatibility building. By figuring out the requirements, inspirations, and worries of others, people can tailor their messages to reverberate with their crowd and cultivate trust and association.

Whether it's convincing a partner to help another drive, persuading a companion to attempt another café, or haggling with a relative on family obligations, the standards of influence are pertinent in a large number of settings. From building agreement and conquering issues with rousing activity and encouraging collaboration, influence can engage people to explore relational elements with elegance and viability.

Yet, influence isn't just about getting what you need; it's additionally about building commonly useful connections in light of trust, regard, and correspondence. By moving toward cooperations with earnestness, honesty, and a certifiable craving to comprehend and uphold others, people can develop significant associations and make positive results for them and everyone around them.

Through a blend of the capacity to understand people on a profound level, relational abilities, and moral influence methods, people can saddle the influential ability to accomplish their targets while reinforcing their connections and adding to a more agreeable and cooperative social climate.

Chapter 6: The Future of Influence and Persuasion

Innovative Progressions

Welcome to the boondocks of impact and influence, where the combination of innovation and brain research is reshaping the manner in which we associate, impart, and simply decide. This segment dives into the interesting domain of innovative progressions and their significant effect on the scene of influence.

Arising advancements like computerized reasoning (man-made intelligence), AI, and augmented reality (VR) are reforming how convincing messages are created, conveyed, and experienced. From customized promoting calculations that designer content to individual inclinations and ways of behaving to vivid VR reproductions that transport clients into influential stories, innovation has opened up new roads for impacting perspectives and ways of behaving on a scale up until recently never envisioned.

In any case, to whom much is given, much will be expected, and the rising refinement of enticing advancements brings up significant moral issues. How would we guarantee that these advancements are utilized capably and morally, without encroaching on individual independence or controlling weak populaces? How would we shield against the potentially negative results of algorithmic predisposition or channel bubbles that build up closed quarters of conviction?

By wrestling with these moral situations and taking part in smart discourse and discussion, we can foster systems for advancing mindful and moral influence rehearses in the computerized age. From straightforwardness and responsibility measures to the improvement of moral rules and norms, there is a lot of work to be finished to guarantee that the force of innovation is bridled for everyone's benefit.

As we stand on the cusp of another time in influence, it is fundamental that we approach these mechanical progressions with modesty, premonition, and a guarantee to maintaining the standards of honesty, straightforwardness, and regard for human pride. Really at that time could we at any point outfit the maximum capacity of innovation to engage, edify, and rouse positive change in our general public.

Moral Contemplations

In the steadily developing scene of impact and influence, moral contemplations pose a potential threat, looking long and hard at a basic eye on the moral difficulties presented by the rising refinement of influence methods. This segment dives into the complex moral territory of influence, examining the potential for abuse or control and talking about procedures for advancing capable and moral influence rehearses.

As influential advances become progressively complex, questions emerge about the moral limits of influence. How would we guarantee that powerful messages are not tricky or manipulative? How would we safeguard weak populaces, like youngsters or those with restricted computerized proficiency, from unjustifiable impact or double-dealing? These inquiries request smart thought and proactive measures to defend against possible damages.

One way to deal with tending to these moral worries is through straightforwardness and responsibility. By guaranteeing that people know about the influential methods being utilized and the goals behind them, we can enable them to go with informed choices and oppose unjustifiable impact. Also, laying out clear rules and guidelines for moral influence practices can assist with forestalling misuse and guarantee that influence is led with honesty and regard for individual independence.

In addition, as innovation keeps on progressing, continuous discourse and cooperation between partners — including policymakers, industry pioneers, scientists, and common society associations — are fundamental for recognizing arising moral difficulties and creating compelling arrangements. By cooperating to advance moral norms and best practices, we can cultivate a culture of capable influence that focuses on the prosperity and independence of people.

Eventually, moral influence isn't simply a question of consistence with guidelines or adherence to rules; it is an ethical basic established in standards of regard, sympathy, and respectability. By maintaining these standards and taking a stab at moral greatness in influence, we can tackle the force of impact to encourage positive results and add to an all the more and evenhanded society.

Mental Bits of knowledge

Inside the profundities of mental exploration lie significant bits of knowledge into the instruments of impact and influence, enlightening the fundamental drivers of human way of behaving and independent direction. This segment dives into state of the art research in brain research and social science, investigating the most recent discoveries and their suggestions for understanding and tackling the influential ability.

Mental exploration has revealed a huge number of elements that impact how we see and answer powerful messages. From the job of feelings and mental predispositions in molding our perspectives and ways of behaving to the effect of normal practices and character on our weakness to influence, these experiences offer a mother lode of information for communicators looking to create more viable and moral enticing procedures.

One area exceptionally compelling is the investigation of influence elements inside internet based conditions, where computerized advancements have changed the manner in which we convey and connect. From the viral spread of deception via virtual entertainment to the customized suggestions produced by algorithmic frameworks, understanding the mental systems at play in computerized influence is fundamental for exploring the undeniably complicated scene of online impact.

Besides, mental exploration has revealed insight into the potential for influence to be utilized as a power for good, cultivating conduct change and advancing positive results in regions like wellbeing, schooling, and natural supportability. By tackling bits of knowledge from brain research, communicators can plan mediations that resound with their crowd's qualities, inspirations, and yearnings, improving the probability of influence achievement.

As we keep on unwinding the secrets of human brain science and conduct, the potential for influence to shape perspectives, convictions, and activities stays as huge and significant as anyone might think possible. By embracing the bits of knowledge gathered from mental exploration and applying them mindfully and morally, we can saddle the influential ability to make positive change in our reality.

Engaging People

In the midst of the intricacies of impact and influence, lies the strengthening of people — the acknowledgment that every individual has the ability to basically assess powerful messages and pursue informed choices. This segment digs into the significance of engaging people to become shrewd and knowing buyers of influence, furnishing them with the information and abilities to explore the enticing scene with certainty and uprightness.

Enabling people starts with encouraging media education and decisive reasoning abilities — furnishing people with the instruments they need to assess the validity, exactness, and purpose behind powerful messages. By helping people to address suppositions, examine proof, and consider elective perspectives, we can immunize them against the inconspicuous strategies of control and influence.

In addition, enabling people includes encouraging mindfulness and the capacity to understand anyone on a deeper level — assisting people with perceiving their own weaknesses and predispositions, and how these might be taken advantage of by enticing messages. By developing a more prominent comprehension of their own qualities, inspirations, and objectives, people can settle on decisions that line up with their bona fide selves, instead of surrendering to outside tensions or impacts.

Moreover, engaging people implies advancing organization and independence — empowering people to play a functioning job in forming their own convictions and ways of behaving, as opposed to latently tolerating the directs of others. By cultivating a feeling of strengthening and self-viability, people can oppose unnecessary impact and declare their own independence notwithstanding convincing messages.

At last, the objective of enabling people is to develop a general public of educated, drew in, and independent residents who are fit for exploring the intricacies of the cutting edge world with certainty and uprightness. By furnishing people with the information, abilities, and backing they need to oppose control and settle on choices that mirror their own qualities and interests, we can make a stronger and majority rule society where the influential ability is used capably and morally.

Conclusion:

Recap of Key Experiences

As we bring our investigation of impact and influence to a nearby, it's fundamental to return to the critical experiences and ideas that have been revealed all through our excursion. This part fills in as a complete recap, refining the most notable focuses and examples found out about the brain science of impact and influence.

All through the book, we've dove into the complexities of human way of behaving and direction, uncovering the bunch factors that shape how we see and answer enticing messages. From the job of mental predispositions and normal practices to the impact of feelings and character, we've acquired a more profound comprehension of the mental components at play in influence.

We've additionally analyzed the viable utilizations of influence in different spaces, from showcasing and publicizing to exchange, governmental issues, and individual cooperations. By investigating true models and contextual analyses, we've perceived how influence methods are utilized to accomplish explicit targets and drive significant results.

Besides, our investigation has not been restricted to the present however has reached out into the future, taking into account the expected ramifications of arising advances and moral contemplations for the act of influence. We've wrestled with the moral issues presented by the rising refinement of influence procedures and talked about methodologies for advancing dependable and moral influence rehearses in the present mind boggling and interconnected world.

Generally speaking, our process has been a rich embroidery of experiences and disclosures, offering significant examples for exploring the influential scene with respectability and viability. As we push ahead, let us convey these bits of knowledge with us, applying them nicely and morally to advance positive change and enable people to settle on informed choices that mirror their qualities and yearnings.

Reflection on Moral Contemplations

In our investigation of impact and influence, we can't neglect the basic significance of moral contemplations. All through the sections, we've experienced various cases where influence methods can be utilized to control, mislead, or take advantage of people for individual addition or detestable purposes.

As we think about the moral elements of influence, we are helped to remember the significant obligation that accompanies employing the ability to impact others. Influence isn't simply an instrument for accomplishing our own targets; it is a method for molding mentalities, ways of behaving, and even characters. With this power comes an ethical basic to guarantee that our influential endeavors are directed with honesty, regard, and thought for the prosperity of others.

We've wrestled with inquiries concerning the limits of influence — where does genuine influence end, and control start? How would we guarantee that enticing messages tell the truth, straightforward, and aware of individual independence? These are difficult inquiries to address, yet they are fundamental for directing our lead as moral communicators.

Additionally, we've thought about the more extensive cultural ramifications of influence, especially in the time of advanced media and algorithmic control. As innovation keeps on progressing, so too do the valuable open doors for influence — and the potential for misuse. From the multiplication of deception and phony news to the disintegration of protection and independence, the moral difficulties presented by influential advances are complex and complex.

As we wrestle with these moral situations, it's vital for approach them with modesty, sympathy, and a pledge to moral greatness. By encouraging a culture of capable influence and moral initiative, we can guarantee that influence is employed as a power for good, advancing positive change and enabling people to pursue informed choices that line up with their qualities and interests.

Source of inspiration

As we finish up our investigation of impact and influence, we are invigorated — to apply the information and bits of knowledge acquired from our excursion to turn out to be more educated and knowing customers regarding influential messages.

Furnished with a more profound comprehension of the mental systems at play in influence, we have the ability to explore the convincing scene with more noteworthy mindfulness and respectability. We can basically assess the messages we experience, investigate their sources, and think about their expectations prior to deciding.

In addition, we are engaged to oppose control and unjustifiable impact, declare our independence, and pursue decisions that line up with our qualities and desires. By developing a feeling of organization and self-viability, we can become dynamic members in molding our own predeterminations, as opposed to latent beneficiaries of powerful messages.

However, our obligation doesn't end there. We are additionally called to be problem solvers — to advance capable and moral influence rehearses in our networks, work environments, and society at large. By showing others how its done, supporting for straightforwardness and responsibility, and cultivating a culture of moral greatness, we can assist with making an existence where influence is used capably and morally to advance positive change and enable people.

In this soul of activity and promotion, let us subscribe to the genuinely trustworthy standards, regard, and sympathy in the entirety of our powerful undertakings. Together, we can saddle the influential ability to make a more brilliant, more impartial future for us and ages to come.

Vision for What's in store

As we plan ahead for impact and influence, let us imagine a reality where influence is employed dependably and morally to advance positive change and enable people.

In this future, influence isn't utilized as a device for control or double-dealing however as a power for good — a method for rousing activity, encouraging sympathy, and building spans across separates.

Influence turns into a cooperative undertaking, grounded in standards of uprightness, straightforwardness, and regard for human nobility.

In this future, people are furnished with the information, abilities, and office to explore the enticing scene with certainty and wisdom. They are basic masterminds and informed leaders, fit for opposing unjustifiable impact and going with decisions that mirror their qualities and yearnings.

In this future, innovation fills in as an impetus for positive change, enhancing the voices of underestimated networks, and engaging people to advocate for civil rights and fairness. Algorithmic frameworks are planned in view of moral standards, focusing on reasonableness, responsibility, and human prosperity.

In this future, influence isn't simply a necessary evil however a device for building a more comprehensive, sympathetic, and feasible world. It is utilized to address squeezing cultural difficulties, from environmental change and imbalance to political polarization and social shamefulness.

As we endeavor towards this vision for the future, let us stay resolute in our obligation to moral greatness and mindful authority in influence. Allow us to cooperate to make a reality where influence is a power for positive change, enabling people to shape their own fates and construct a more promising time to come for all.